START UP BUSINESS: HOW TO START UP YOUR BUSINESS TODAY, A COMPLETE GUIDE FOR BEGINNERS

Book 1

By Ellis Mitchell

Why I wrote this book?

I wrote this book because Building a successful enterprise while also fostering strong family ties presents unique challenges. The entrepreneur cannot measure success by financial gains alone, but must consider personal satisfaction and a well-balanced family life as well.

My new serial books "START UP BUSINESS" can help you to get the healthy Balance between Business and Family Life to Achieve True Wealth and Happiness is a book for all entrepreneurs—both waiting-to-be entrepreneurs contemplating the idea of striking out on their own and those already involved in running their own businesses. If you are considering the possibility of launching your own company, I offer encouragement; if you have vision and the willingness to work hard at something about which you are passionate, you too can succeed as an entrepreneur. If you have recently become an entrepreneur, this book will help you to draft a blueprint for your own career.

Throughout this account of my career, I stop on occasion to point out lessons I have learned from my experiences. You will see that they are very basic and fundamental.

This is not the first book by a successful entrepreneur that offers advice by sharing personal successes and failures, and points out lessons that can help readers chart a course to financial and personal success. Numerous books have been written by academics and business entrepreneurs that lay out business theory, occasionally citing cases that support their approach to business management and development.

I hope you will let me show you how you, too, can become an entrepreneur, achieving success in business as well as in family life. The rewards can go far beyond the accumulation of material wealth.

Why you should read this book?

1. You should read this book if you need to:
2. Understand the concept of START UP BUSNIESS and what is the specific criteria that control the success of your new business
3. Avoid the mistakes that many of the new Entrepreneurs falls in at and after the start-up stage
4. Know more about the Entrepreneurs profile, characteristics, personalities, and needed skills.
5. Realize the benefits and opportunities behind owning a small business.
6. Learn how to avoid the main draw backs facing the Entrepreneurs.
7. Understand the culture diversity of the Entrepreneurs

Table of contents:

Why I wrote this book?

Why you should read this book?

Table of contents:

About the Author

Other books by Michelle Thomas

One last thing:

I. Let's start it up

II. Who is an entrepreneur?

III. Benefits and opportunities behind ownership of small business

IV. Potential Negatives of entrepreneurship

V. Why Prosperity? The Fuel Feeding the Entrepreneurial Fire

VI. The Diversity of Entrepreneurship culture

VII. The Importance of Small Business

VII. Ten Deadly Mistakes don't ever do if you want to be an Entrepreneurship

IX. Consider Failure for success

X. How to avoid the Traps?

10 Important points to Remember

Book summery

Action Plan "Bonus"

About the Author

A young self-motivated Author with Great Entrepreneurship experience in several countries.

Started his journey about 30 years back and now he is one of the well know Entrepreneurs in the world.

Other books by Ellis Mitchell

Coming soon START UP BUSINESS Book2

One last thing:

If you enjoyed this book or find it useful, I'd be very grateful if you would post short review on Amazon, your support really does make a difference and I read all of the reviews personally so I can get your feedback and make that book even better.

If you would like to give a review, then all you need to do is click the reviewer link on this book's page on Amazon here

Thanks again for your support.

Let's Get Started!!!

I. Let's start it up

A. The dramatic resurgence of the entrepreneurial spirit:

1. In the U.S. Business Start-Ups found that 8 million people, or one in 25 adults, were actively engaged in trying to launch a new business.

2. This resurgence of the entrepreneurial spirit is the most significant economic development in recent business history.

3. Entrepreneurs have introduced innovative products and services, pushed back technological frontiers, created new jobs, opened foreign markets.

4. So, they sparked the U.S. economy into regaining its competitive edge in the world.

5. In 1969, entrepreneurs created 274,000 new corporations; few years back, the number of new incorporations exceeds 800,000 per year, can you predict what is the number now!!!

6. In a recent survey of college seniors, 49 percent of the men and 31 percent of the women said they were interested in pursuing entrepreneurship when they graduate.

B. It is now much easier than ever to launch of new business:

1. Due to new technological developments, it is possible for companies to accomplish more with fewer people. As a result, people who once saw launching a business as being too risky now see it as the ideal way to create their own job security.

2. Although launching a business is never easy, the resources available today make the job much simpler today than ever before since thousands of colleges and universities offer courses in entrepreneurship.

3. Internet hosts a sea of information on launching a business including sources of capital.

4. Another significant shift in growth of small company has been due to significant shift in our nation's economic structure

(rapidly moving away from an industrial economy to a knowledge-based one).

II. Who is an entrepreneur?

A. Definition

An entrepreneur is one who creates a new business in the face of risk and uncertainty for the purpose of achieving profit and growth opportunities and assembles the necessary resources to capitalize on those opportunities.

B. Choosing entrepreneurship:

1. Have been downsized or laid off   5%
2. Wanted to fulfil lifelong goal   25%
3. Tired of working for someone else   27%
4. Wanted more control over future   36%
5. Joined family business   41%

C. Entrepreneurial profile

1. Taking responsibility

They prefer to be in control of their resources and to use those resources to achieve self-determined goals.

2. Moderate risk taker

Entrepreneurs are not wild risk-takers, but are instead calculating risk-takers.

3. High Confidence in success

They need to be optimistic about the chances for success.

4. Always ask for feedback

Entrepreneurs like to know how they are doing and are constantly looking for reinforcement.

5. Highly energetic

Entrepreneurs are more energetic than the average person. Typically, they work long hours, often 60 to 80 hours a week.

6. Optimistic

Entrepreneurs tend to dream big and then formulate plans to transfer those dreams into reality.

7. Skilful

Entrepreneurs know how to put the right people and resources together to accomplish a task.

8. Calculate ROI (Return On Investment)

Achievements seems to be the primary motivating force behind entrepreneurs - money is simply a way of keeping score off accomplishments.

D. Other characteristics

1. Highly committed

An Entrepreneur's commitment to his or her and the business it spawns determines how successful his or her company ultimately becomes.

2. Tolerance for ambiguity

Entrepreneurs tend to have a high tolerance for ambiguous, ever-changing situations.

3. Flexible

Entrepreneurs must be willing to adapt their businesses to meet changes.

4. Tenacity

Successful entrepreneurs have the willpower to conquer the barriers that stand in the way of their success.

E. The 5 different entrepreneurial personalities:

1. Initiator with new ideas

Idealists started their businesses because they had a great idea or wanted to work on something special.

Idealists enjoy creative work but are impatient with performing administrative tasks such as financial analysis or legal matters.

This group of entrepreneurs and their businesses are most dependent on computers.

2. Optimizers

Optimizers (28% of all entrepreneurs) are the second largest category.

The benefits of entrepreneurship are most important to them; they enjoy the freedom and flexibility of owning a business and would not be willing to work for someone else.

They want their companies to grow, but their focus is on profits rather than on revenues.

These business owners are highly knowledgeable about financial issues and use technology to keep costs down and productivity up.

They worry less than other business owners because they see themselves as maintaining control over their businesses.

They also have learned the secrets of balancing their home and business lives.

3. Working hard

Hard workers make up 20% of the entrepreneurial population.

They love their work and are more likely than any other group to put in extra hours to achieve the targets.

They tend to be detail-oriented and are the most growth-oriented entrepreneurial group.

They are financially aggressive and exercise broad control over the details of running their businesses.

Hard workers typically have long-term business plans and stick to them.

4. Jugglers

Jugglers also make up 20 percent of the entrepreneurial population.

They have a difficult time delegating authority and responsibility.

They prefer to do things themselves to make sure everything meets their high standards.

They are highly energetic people who are good at handling multiple tasks simultaneously.

They readily embrace technology in their companies and are always looking for ways to improve their businesses.

Jugglers feel pressure to maintain positive cash flow in their companies.

5. Sustains

Sustains person comprise 15 percent of all entrepreneurs

These entrepreneurs are more likely to have inherited or bought their companies.

They are the least comfortable with technology and prefer to put in more time than to figure out how to apply technology to solve a particular problem.

sustains are the most conservative group and do not strive to achieve significant levels of growth.

Maintaining a good balance between business and home life is important to them.

III. Benefits and opportunities behind ownership of small business

A. Opportunity to control your own destiny

1. Owning a business.
2. Rewards of knowing you are the driving forces behind their businesses.

B. Opportunity to make a difference

1. Opportunity to do what is important to you.

C. Opportunity to reach your full potential

1. Escape from boring and unchallenging work.
2. Entrepreneurship is a vehicle for self-expression.

D. Opportunity to get unlimited profits

1. Money is not the primary motivator, but owning your own business is a great way to create wealth.
2. Typical American millionaire is first-generation wealthy, owns a small business and works 45-55 hours a week.

E. Opportunity to contribute to society and be recognized for your efforts

1. Often small business owners are among the most trusted and respected members of their communities.
2. Entrepreneurs enjoy the recognition they get from customers for doing a job well.

F.   Opportunity to make your hobby to be your job

1.   Their work is not really work; it's their avocation turned into a vocation.

IV. Potential Negatives of entrepreneurship

A. Uncertainty of income

1. The regularity of income from working for someone is gone.

2. "The entrepreneur is the last one to be paid."

B. Risk of losing your entire money

1. 34% fail within 2 years.

2. 50% shut down within 4 years.

3. 60% fold within 6 years.

4. Consider the risk-reward trade-off

a) What is the worst thing that could happen if my business fails?

b) How likely is it that the worst to happen?

c) What can I do to lower the risk that my business will fail?

d) What is my contingency plan for coping if my business fails?

C. Long hours and hard work

1. 10- to 12-hour days and six- or seven-day workweeks with no paid vacations.

2. Owners experience intense, draining workdays.

D. Have Low quality of life until the business gets established

The workload can take a toll on the entrepreneur's personal life and family.

Most launch their business when they are between 25 and 34, just as their families are starting.

E. Highly stressed

- Running your own business is highly stressful.
- Failure can mean total financial ruin.

F. Complete responsibility

Entrepreneurs end up taking on issues with which they are not knowledgeable.

The owner is the business.

G. Discouragement

- Requires much dedication, discipline, and tenacity.
- Entrepreneurs will run headlong into many obstacles, some of which may appear to be insurmountable.
- Discouragement and disillusionment can set in.

V. Why Prosperity? The Fuel Feeding the Entrepreneurial Fire

A. Entrepreneurs as heroes

> Americans have very positive attitudes towards entrepreneurs.

B. Entrepreneurial education

> More colleges and universities are offering courses; more students see entrepreneurship as a career option.
>
> 4000 colleges and universities offer courses to 50,000 students.

C. Demographic and economic factors

> Most start their businesses between ages 25 to 44.

D. Shift to a service economy

> By 2018, the service sector will produce 94 % of the jobs and 86 %of the GDP in the U.S.
>
> The booming service sector has provided entrepreneurs with many business opportunities.

E. Technological advancements

> Make it easier for entrepreneurs to start and run a business, faxes, computers, voice mail, etc.

F. Independent lifestyles

> Entrepreneurship fits the American life, independence and self-sufficiency.

G. The World Wide Web (WW)

H. International opportunities

1. 95% of the world's population lives outside of U.S. borders.
2. Small businesses account for 96 percent of all exporters; however, they account for just 20 percent of total exports.
3. Richard Allred story

   Richard Allred launched a company that produces surf-related clothing and apparel. Toes on the Nose Corporation domestic sales grew quickly, but Allred also saw opportunities to sell his products in foreign markets such as Australia, Canada, Great Britain, and Japan.

VI. The Diversity of Entrepreneurship culture

A. Young Entrepreneurs

1. Generation X, people born between 1965 and 1980, is the most entrepreneurial generation in history.
2. Members of this generation are responsible for 70 percent of all business start-ups!
3. Recent surveys have found that 60 percent of 18-to 29-year-olds say they hope to launch their own businesses.
4. "Generation X" might be more appropriately called "Generation E."

B. Women Entrepreneurs

1. Small business has been a leader in offering women opportunities for economic expression through employment and entrepreneurship.
2. Increasing numbers of women are discovering that the best way to break the "glass ceiling" that prevents them from rising to the top of many organizations is to start their own companies (see Figure 1.3).
3. Women are opening businesses at a rate twice that of the national average
4. Women are launching businesses in fields that traditionally have been male-dominated.
5. The 9.8 million women-owned companies across the United States employ 36.4 million workers, about 20 percent of all company workers in the country.
6. Women own about 38 percent of all businesses, and these companies generate approximately $5.1 trillion in sales each year.

C. Minority Enterprises

1. Asians, Hispanics, and African-Americans, respectively, are most likely to become entrepreneurs.

2. Like women, minorities cite discrimination as a principal reason for their limited access to the world of entrepreneurship.
3. Studies show that the nation's minority entrepreneurs own 4.3 million businesses that generate $573 billion in revenues and employ nearly 4 million workers.

D. **Immigrant Entrepreneurs**

E. **Many are lured to the U.S. by its economic freedom.**

Come with few assets but lots of drive and dreams.

F. **Part-time entrepreneurs**

Permits people to try it with low-risk.
about18 million Americans are self-employed part-time.

G. **Home-based business owners**

1. 57% of all businesses are home-based, but about 80 percent of them are very small with no employees.
2. Study reported more than 63,000 home-based businesses generating sales of more than $1 million per year.
3. The biggest advantage is the cost savings of not having to lease or buy an external location.
4. They also enjoy the benefits of flexible work and lifestyles.

19important home-based entrepreneurs should follow:

1. Managing a Successful Home-Based Business.
2. Do your homework
3. Find out what your zoning restrictions are
4. Choose the most efficient location for your office
5. Focus your home-based business idea
6. Discuss your business rules with your family
7. Select an appropriate business name
8. Buy the right equipment
9. Dress appropriately

10. Learn to deal with distractions
11. Realize that your phone can be your best friend ... or your worst enemy
12. Be firm with friends and neighbours
13. Take advantage of tax breaks
14. Make sure you have adequate insurance coverage
15. Understand the special circumstances under which you can hire outside employees
16. Be prepared if your business requires clients to come to your home
17. Get a post office box
18. Network, network, network
19. Be proud of your home-based business

H. Family business owners

1. Of the 25.5 million businesses in the United States, 90% are family-owned and managed.
2. These companies account for 60 % of total employment in the United States and generate more than 50% of the U.S. Gross Domestic Product (GDP).
3. 37% of the Fortune 500 companies are family businesses.
4. Only 33% of family businesses survive to the second generation; just 12% make it to the third generation; and only 3% survive to the fourth generation and beyond.

I. Co-preneurs

1. Entrepreneurial couples who work together as co-owners of their businesses.
2. Companies co-owned by spouses represent one of the fastest growing business sectors.
3. Some of the characteristics they rely on include:
4. personalities that mesh.
5. mutual respect.
6. compatible goals.
7. equal partnership.
8. complementary business skills.
9. open communication.
10. clear division of roles and authority.
11. ability to encourage each other.
12. separate work spaces.
13. boundaries between work and personal life.

14. a sense of humour.
15. may not work with every couple.

J. Corporate castoffs

1. As major U.S. companies have "trimmed their ranks," many of these displaced workers have launched their own companies.
2. 20% of these managers start their own companies.
3. An entrepreneurial offense is the best defence to corporate layoffs.

K. Corporate dropouts

1. Downsizing has diminished employee loyalties.
2. Many are striking out on their own for more opportunity, better income, and more "job security."

VII. The Importance of Small Business

A. Introduction

1. 37.2 million businesses, 98.5% of all businesses in the U.S. would qualify as small businesses.
2. Small business employs more than 52% of the private sector work force.
3. Virtually all job growth in 1990s came from small business, creating 75.8% of new jobs.
4. Small companies bear the heaviest load of training new workers.
5. Small businesses produce 54% of the GDP and 49% of business sales.
6. They also generate 22% more innovations per employee than large companies.

VII. Ten Deadly Mistakes don't ever do if you want to be an Entrepreneurship

A. Small businesses have a much higher failure rate than larger businesses.

1. 60% will fail in six years.
2. Causes of small business failure
   limited resources, inexperienced management, and lack of financial stability.

B. Poor Managerial skills

1. Management inexperience or poor decision making ability is the chief problem of the failing enterprise.
2. The owner-leader lacks the knowledge or ability needed.

C. Undercapitalization

1. Any successful business venture requires proper financial control.
2. Two pitfalls affecting small business's financial health are common: undercapitalization and poor cash management.
3. Entrepreneurs tend to be overly optimistic and often underestimate the financial requirements of launching a business or the amount of time required for the company to become self-sustaining.

D. Poor Cash Control

1. Insufficient cash flow due to poor cash management is a common cause of business failure.
2. Maintaining adequate cash flow to pay bills in a timely fashion is a constant challenge for small companies.
3. Poor credit and collection practices on accounts receivable, sloppy accounts payable practices that exert undue pressure on a company's cash balance, and uncontrolled spending are common to many small business bankruptcies.

E. Lack of Strategic Management capabilities

1. Too many small business managers neglect the process of strategic management.
2. Failure to plan, however, usually results in failure to survive.
3. Clearly defined strategy is necessary for creating and maintaining a competitive edge.
4. Building a strategic plan forces an entrepreneur to assess realistically the proposed business's potential.

F. Weak Marketing Activities

Sometimes entrepreneurs believe that if they "build it," customers automatically "will come."

G. Uncontrolled growth

1. They will outgrow their capital base with every 40 to 50% increase in sales.
2. Ideally the business should expand on retained earnings.
3. Growth also requires structural and other changes.
4. The most important change occurs in managerial expertise.

H. Pad location

1. Location is part art and part science.
2. Owners need to investigate before they locate.
   It's critical in retail.
3. Keys to location.
   What it costs.
   What it generates in sales volume.

I. Lack of Inventory Control

1. Inventory control is one of the most neglected areas in small business.
2. Insufficient inventory levels result in shortages and stock outs causing customers to become disillusioned and not return.
3. Has too much inventory or has too much of the wrong type of inventory.

J. Not able to Make the "Entrepreneurial Transition."

1. Many businesses fail when their founders are unable to make the transition from entrepreneur to manager and are unwilling to bring in a professional management team.
2. Growth requires entrepreneurs to delegate authority.
3. They should avoid micromanaging.

IX. Consider Failure for success

1. It is a natural part of the process. The only way to not fail is to not do anything.
2. Learn from failures and be more successful the next time. It's not mistake avoidance but learning from mistakes that counts.
3. Entrepreneurship requires persistence and resilience.

X. How to avoid the Traps?

A. Know your business well

1. Get the best education and experience before you start.

B. Be ready with your Business Plan

1. Planning replaces "I think" with "I know."
2. Most entrepreneurs don't have a solid plan.
3. Entrepreneurs attempt to build businesses on faulty assumptions.

C. Control Financial Resources

1. Develop a practical information system and use it to make decisions.
2. To have adequate start-up capital.
3. Estimate capital needed then double it.
4. Cash is your most valuable resource.

D. Understand Financial Statements

1. These documents are reliable indicators of the small business's health. Know them.
2. Know the financial danger signs to look for.

E. Learn more about People Managementin an Effective way

1. Your hires will determine where your company will go.
2. Share information.

F. Set your business apart from the competition

1. Differentiate your company and products.
2. Convince your customers that you are different from competitors.

3. For small companies, that basis often is customer service, convenience, speed, quality, or whatever else is important to attracting and keeping happy customers.

G. Keep in tune with yourself.

1. Requires lots of energy and enthusiasm.
2. Manage yourself.
3. Keep a positive attitude.
4. Keep your passion.

10 Important points to Remember

1. **The importance of the entrepreneur in business in the United States and across the globe**

   Record numbers of people have launched companies over the past decade. The boom in entrepreneurship is not limited solely to the United States; many nations across the globe are seeing similar growth in the small business sector. A variety of competitive, economic, and demographic shifts have created a world in which "small is beautiful."
   Society depends on entrepreneurs to provide the drive and risk-taking necessary for the business system to supply people with the goods and services they need.

2. **The entrepreneur characteristics**

   Entrepreneurs have some common characteristics, including a desire for responsibility, a preference for moderate risk, confidence in their ability to succeed, a desire for immediate feedback, a high energy level, a future orientation, skill at organizing, and a value of achievement over money. In a phrase, they are high achievers.

3. **Benefits and opportunities of owning a small business**

   Driven by these personal characteristics, entrepreneurs establish and manage small businesses to gain control over their lives, become self-fulfilled, reap unlimited profits, contribute to society, and do what they enjoy doing.

4. **The potential risks of owning a small business**

   Small business ownership has some potential drawbacks. There are no guarantees that the business will make a profit or even survive. The time and energy required to manage a new business may have dire effects on the owner and family members.

5. Growth driving forces of entrepreneurship

    Several factors are driving the boom in entrepreneurship, including the portrayal of entrepreneurs as heroes, better entrepreneurial education, economic and demographic factors, a shift to a service economy, technological advancements, more-independent lifestyles, and increased international opportunities.

6. Role of diversity in small business

    Several groups are leading the nation's drive toward entrepreneurship: women, minorities, immigrants, "part-timers," home-based business owners, family business owners, co-preneurs, corporate castoffs, and corporate dropouts.

7. Contributions small businesses make to the U.S. economy

    The small business sector's contributions are many. They make up 99 percent of all businesses, employ 53 percent of the private sector workforce, create 75.8% of the new jobs in the economy, produce 51 percent of the country's private Gross Domestic Product (GDP), and account for 47 percent of business sales.

8. Reasons of fail

    The failure rate for small businesses is higher than for big businesses, and profits fluctuate with general economic conditions. SBA statistics show that 60 percent of new businesses will have failed within six years. The primary cause of business failure is incompetent management. Other reasons include poor financial control, failure to plan, inappropriate location, lack of inventory control, improper managerial attitudes, and inability to make the "entrepreneurial transition."

9. business failure into the proper perspective

    Because they are building businesses in an environment filled with uncertainty and shaped by rapid change, entrepreneurs recognize that failure is likely to be a part of their lives; yet, they are not paralysed by that fear. Successful entrepreneurs have the attitude that failures are simply stepping stones along the path to success.

10. Avoid the major pitfalls of running a business.

There are several general tactics the small business owner can employ to avoid failure. The entrepreneur should know the business in depth, develop a solid business plan, manage financial resources effectively, understand financial statements, learn to manage people effectively, set the business apart from the competition, and keep in tune with yourself.

Book summery

1. **Forces have led to the growth in entrepreneurship in the United States**

    Corporate downsizing flooding the market with corporate cast-offs, an attitude that small is beautiful, international economic development due to the fall of communism and the "capitalization" of former state-owned industries, a dream of freedom and independence, perseverance in achieving results, and the opportunities presented by an ever-changing environment.

2. **Entrepreneurial profile**

    One who creates a new business in the face of risk and uncertainty for the purpose of achieving profit and growth by identifying opportunities and assembling the necessary resources to capitalize on them. Profile - a) desire for responsibility, b) preference for moderate risk, c) confidence in personal success, d) desire for immediate feedback, e) high level of energy, f) possess a future orientation, g) skill in organization, h) money is a great way to keep score but it is not as important as achievement.

3. **Major benefits of business ownership**

    a) opportunity to gain control over your destiny
    b) opportunity to make a difference
    c) opportunity to reach your full potential
    d) opportunity to reap unlimited profits
    e) opportunity to make a contribution to society and receive recognition for your efforts.

4. **Potential risks to business ownership are most critical**
    a) uncertainty of income

b) risk of losing invested capital
c) long hours and hard work
d) lower quality of life until the business gets established
e) complete responsibility.

5. **Contributions of businesses make to economy**

There is no set definition of a small business. SBA criteria vary by industry, 98% of U.S. businesses could be considered small. They've contributed almost all of the recent job growth, employ over 50% of the private workforce, and contribute 48% of our GNP and 42% of all business sales.

6. **Small business failure rate**

The failure rate for small businesses is higher than for big businesses. Based on data released from SBA, 60 percent of new businesses fail within six years. The primary reason is incompetent management. Other reasons are poor financial control, failure to plan, inappropriate location, lack of inventory control, improper managerial attitudes, and inability to make the "entrepreneurial transition."

7. **Causes of business failure**

- Management incompetence - This one causes the most problems. The manager lacks the capacity to operate a small business successfully.

- Lack of experience - Many owners who start businesses in fields in which they have no prior experience fail. Some owners lack the right kind of experience.

- Poor financial control - Undercapitalization Starting the business on a "shoestring" -often leads to failure.

- Lack of strategic planning - Too many owners neglect it because they think it only benefits large companies.

- Uncontrolled growth - Growth is natural and healthy, but unplanned growth can be fatal to the business.

- Inappropriate location - Owners who choose a business location without proper analysis, investigation, and planning often fail. Too often, owners seek "cheap" sites and locate themselves straight into failure.

- Lack of inventory control - Although inventory is typically the largest investment for the owner, inventory control is one of the most neglected duties. The result is loss through crime and pressure on cash flows from handling the wrong items.

- Inability to make the "entrepreneurial transition" - Having started the business, some entrepreneurs lack the ability to manage it when it gets larger and fail to turn it over to a different management team.

8. **Avoid the common pitfalls that often lead to business failure**

Doing the following will help to avoid pitfalls.

a) know the business in depth.
b) prepare a business plan.
c) manage financial resources.
d) understand financial statements and know how to use them.
e) learn to manage people effectively.
f) keep in tune with yourself.

9. **Importance of the study the small business failure rate?**

It provides a realistic picture for potential entrepreneurs to consider prior to their launching of their businesses. It provides understanding of why businesses fail and offers insight into ways to prevent it.

10. Typical entrepreneur's attitude toward failure?

He/she learn from the mistakes and tries again. He/she takes moderate, considered risks, has a positive upbeat attitude, and doesn't avoid failure; he/she learn from it.

11. Main advice for your entrepreneurial friend who has just suffered a business failure

should include a reality check, long hours, high failure rate, and a dose of the positive, persist, learn, don't give up.

Action Plan "Bonus"

1. Choose an entrepreneur in your community and interview him or her. What's the "story" behind the business? What advantages and disadvantages does the owner see in owning a business? What advice would he or she offer to someone considering launching a business?

2. Search through recent business publications (especially those focusing on small companies such as Inc., Entrepreneur, Business Start-Ups, Nation's Business, or Your Company) and find an example of an entrepreneur--past or present--who exhibits the entrepreneurial spirit of striving for success in the face of failure as Gail Borden did. Prepare a brief report for your class.

3. Select one of the categories under the section "The Diversity of Entrepreneurship" in this chapter and research it in more detail. Find examples of the entrepreneurial profile. Prepare a brief report for your class.

4. Interview a local banker who has experience lending to small companies. What factors does he or she believe are important to a small company's success? What factors has he or she seen to cause business failures? What does the lender want to see in a business start-up before agreeing to lend any money?

See you in Book 2

<<<End of Book 1>>>

www.ingramcontent.com/pod-product-compliance
Lightning Source LLC
Chambersburg PA
CBHW061235180526
45170CB00003B/1304